DESERT ANIMALS AND PLANTS FOR KIDS

Habitat Facts, Photos and Fun

Children's Environment Books Edition

SPEEDY
PUBLISHING

Speedy Publishing LLC
40 E. Main St. #1156
Newark, DE 19711
www.speedypublishing.com

Desert bighorn sheeps are native to the deserts of the Southwestern United States and Northwestern Mexico.

boa is a
all mammal
t belongs
he group of
ping rodents.
boa has
use-like head
h large eyes
whiskers.

Jerboa inhabits cold and hot deserts of Asia and North Africa.

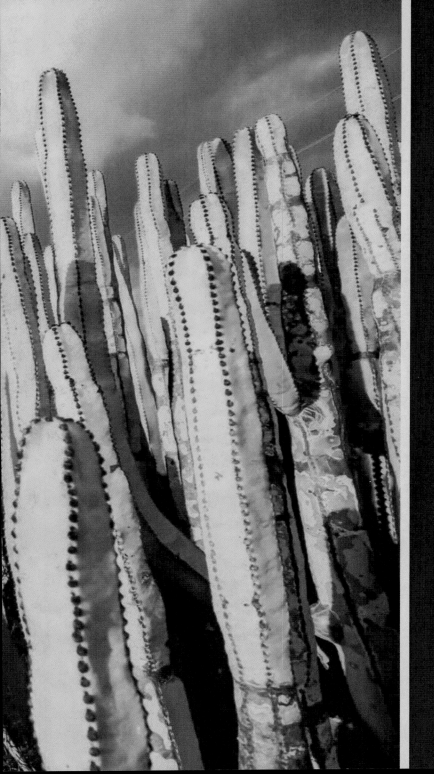

Cactus is a type of plant that can store large amounts of water and survive in extremely hot and dry habitats.

Almost all cacti are native to deserts and dry regions of South and North America.

Brittlebrush is a medium-sized rounded shrub. They grow up up to 30 to 150 centimetres tall.

They can be found in dry gravelly slopes, roadsides, open sandy washes, sage scrub, inland valleys and deserts.

Jumping cholla has tree-like shape. Jumping cholla can reach 6 to 15 feet in height and around 8 feet in diameter.

Jumping cholla
is adapted to
the life in arid
areas. They
can be found
in Sonoran
desert and
southwestern
parts of the USA.

Most desert species have found remarkable ways to survive by evading drought.

Camels are mammals with long legs, a big-lipped snout and a humped back. Camels coats reflect the desert sun and keeps them cool in very hot temperatures.

Camels are usually found in the desert, prairie or steppe.

The desert tortoise is a thick skinned reptile, with a scaly head. The desert tortoises live about 50 to 80 years.

The desert tortoise is native to the Mojave and Sonoran Deserts. They spend most of their time in burrows, rock shelters, and pallets to regulate body temperature and reduce water loss.

Thorny devils are covered from head to tail with spines and thorns. Thorny devils change color depending on the temperature.

Thorny devils
live in the arid
scrubland
and deserts
of Australia.

Armadillo girdled lizards have triangular head and flattened body and tail. Body of armadillo lizards is covered with square-shaped scales.

The Armadillo
Girdled Lizard
can only be
found in the
desert regions
of southern
Africa.
Armadillo lizard
inhabits deserts,
scrublands
and dry,
rocky areas.

The desert bighorn has become well adapted to living in the desert heat and cold and their body temperature can safely fluctuate several degrees.